essential
Chinese

essential
Chinese

hamlyn

First published in Great Britain in 1997 by
Hamlyn a division of Octopus Publishing Group Limited
2-4 Heron Quays, London E14 4JP

Reprinted in 2002

Designed and produced by SP Creative Design
Linden House, Kings Road, Bury St Edmunds, Suffolk, England
Editor and writer: Heather Thomas
Art Director: Al Rockall
Designer: Rolando Ugolini

ISBN 0 600 60590 6

A CIP catalogue record for this book is available from the
British Library

Printed in China

Acknowledgements
Special photography: Phil Webb
Step-by-step photography: GGS Photographics, Norwich
Food preparation: Jo Craig, Dawn Stock and Caroline Stevens
Styling: Helen Payne

Notes
1. Standard spoon measurements are used in all recipes.
1 tablespoon = one 15ml spoon
1 teaspoon = one 5ml spoon

2. Both imperial and metric measurements have been
given in all recipes. Use one set of measurements
only and not a mixture of both.

3. Eggs should be size 3 unless otherwise stated.

4. Milk should be full fat unless otherwise stated.

5. Fresh herbs should be used unless otherwise stated.
If unavailable, use dried herbs as an alternative, but halve
the quantities stated.

6. Ovens should be preheated to the specified temperature. If
using a fan assisted oven, follow the manufacturer's instructions
for adjusting the time and the temperature.

CONTENTS

INTRODUCTION

China is such a vast country that the styles of cuisine and regional dishes are extremely varied and reflect both the changes in climate and geography, and the foods grown. There are four main regional cookery schools: the Eastern School, which includes the fertile Yangtse Basin, Shanghai and the provinces of Jiangsi and Fujian, has many speciality fish and rice dishes. The Southern School is regarded as the jewel of Chinese cuisine and includes Canton and the province of Guangdong. The Western School specializes in spicy, piquant food from Sichuan province, whereas the Northern School is the oldest of the four and encompasses the cuisines of Beijing, Shandong and Henan.

Chinese food is incredibly diverse and can be refined and delicate, or robust and earthy. However, what is common to all Chinese dishes is the necessity of using only the freshest ingredients. Vegetables are often gathered immediately before cooking, and poultry and fish are often bought alive. To the Chinese, loss of freshness means loss of flavour.

A Chinese meal consists of many dishes, all carefully selected so as to complement and balance each other in texture, flavour, shape and colour. It is a very healthy cuisine: many dishes are steamed or quickly stir-fried in the minimum of oil (*ch'ao*). The ingredients to be stir-fried are usually cut into strips or dice so that they cook through quickly and the maximum food surface is in contact with the heat. They are cooked in a wok, a traditional Chinese round-bottomed pan, and are kept in continuous motion as the cook moves and tosses them in the hot oil or sauce. The short cooking time, literally in minutes, helps to preserve the nutrients and natural flavours of food and means that it is eaten really fresh.

The most time-consuming part of creating a Chinese meal, with its range of different dishes, is in its preparation. Many of the ingredients are cut into chunks, shreds, strips, dice or cubes, and elaborate garnishes are sometimes prepared. However, you can do all this in advance earlier in the day and store in the refrigerator until it is time to cook the meal.

Bamboo shoots

These are the tender, edible shoots of certain bamboo plants which are harvested at the end of the rainy season. In China, they may be used fresh or canned. They have a distinctive crunchy texture and are often sliced and added to stir-fried dishes. They are available in cans in Western countries and can be stored in fresh water in the refrigerator for up to seven days after opening.

Bean curd

This is also known as doufu or tofu, and is sold in white blocks. It is extremely healthy and nutritious, being rich in protein and low in fat. Made from puréed yellow soy beans, it has a bland flavour and is often used in soups and stir-fries. Fresh bean curd can be covered and kept in the refrigerator for several days.

Bean sprouts

These are the crisp, crunchy sprouts of mung or soy beans. They are an essential

ingredient in many stir-fried and savoury dishes. They can be kept in the salad crisper compartment of a refrigerator.

Black beans

These small fermented black soy beans have a salty flavour and are often ground into a paste and mixed with spices before being bottled as black bean sauce.

Chillies

Both fresh and dried chillies are used in Chinese food. Fiery fresh red ones are widely used in the western and northern regions, whereas dried chillies are common in spicy Sichuan food. Chillies are used to flavour cooking oils, are ground into powder and may be made into a variety of sauces. Chilli dipping sauce is fiery and a brilliant red, and is usually made from chillies, vinegar, salt and sugar.

Always take care when handling fresh chillies. Wear protective gloves or wash your hands thoroughly afterwards. Avoid contact with your eyes and delicate skin as the seeds can burn you.

Chinese mushrooms

These fragrant dried mushrooms have a distinctive smoky flavour and are sold in many delicatessens and Chinese speciality stores. They must be soaked and reconstituted in warm water before cooking; the stems are discarded.

Coriander

Together with chives, this is the herb that is most commonly used in Chinese cookery. Sometimes referred to as Chinese parsley, it is used to flavour and garnish many fish and chicken dishes.

Cornflour

This is widely used as a thickening agent in sauces and batters, and in marinades to coat such foods as chicken, pork and prawns. It is always blended with cold water, Chinese wine or other liquids before being added to a sauce.

Five-spice powder

This is a fragrant mixture of ground star anise, spicy Sichuan peppercorns, fennel, cloves and cinnamon. It is used to flavour many Chinese savoury dishes, especially red-cooked meat and poultry.

Flour

In China, flour may be made with wheat, ground raw rice or glutinous rice. Rice flour is often used to make the dough for dim sum (snack) dumplings.

Ginger root

Sometimes called green ginger, fresh ginger root is used widely to flavour soups, meat, fish and vegetable dishes. It must be peeled before using and is then sliced, chopped or crushed. If you wish to keep ginger fresh for several months, you can peel it and preserve in a screwtop jar filled with sherry or rice wine. The ginger can then be used as required, and the sherry will be infused with a marvellous ginger flavour and can be added to many dishes. The Chinese have a sweet tooth and also use crystallized stem ginger in many desserts.

Hoisin sauce

This thick dark brown sauce is made from soy beans, sugar, flour, garlic, chillies, vinegar, salt and sesame seed oil. It is sold in jars and is available in supermarkets. It is often used to marinate meat, and is sometimes known as barbecue sauce.

Lychees

These delicately flavoured fruit are beloved of the Chinese and appear in our shops at Christmas-time. The fragrant white flesh is enclosed in a hard pink shell, which can be peeled away. They can be bought in cans all the year round.

Noodles

These are eaten at nearly all Chinese meals and may be made from wheat, sometimes enriched with egg, or rice, or ground mung beans (transparent or cellophane noodles). They may be purchased dried or fresh and there are many varieties.

Rice noodles should be soaked in warm water until they are soft and then they may be stir-fried with vegetables or added to soups and other cooked dishes. Transparent noodles are available dried and are soaked before using. They are often deep-fried.

Oils

These may be made either from corn, sunflowers, rapeseed, soybeans, cottonseed, peanuts or sesame seeds. They are used in stir-frying and deep-frying as well as to flavour food. The most distinctive and strongly flavoured is sesame oil, which is often used in marinades or may be sprinkled on savoury dishes immediately

before serving. Oils are often flavoured with aromatics and fiery chillies.

Oyster sauce

This is a common ingredient in Cantonese cooking. Although it is made from oysters and soy sauce, surprisingly it does not have a fishy flavour.

Rice

Who could imagine a Chinese meal without rice? Long-grain, short-grain and glutinous varieties are all used. Glutinous rice has a sticky texture and is often cooked wrapped in lotus leaves. In China, rice is always washed several times in clean water before cooking.

Rice wine

This is used in cooking, especially in marinades and sauces, as well as for drinking. If you cannot obtain it, a dry sherry will make an adequate substitute.

Sesame seeds

Dried sesame seeds are used for flavouring many dishes. Sometimes the seeds are lightly toasted or roasted before using. They may also be used for making sesame oil, or ground into paste.

Soy sauce

This is an essential ingredient in Chinese cookery. It is made from fermented soy beans and may be light or dark in colour. Light soy sauce has a salty flavour and is considered superior to dark soy sauce.

Star anise

This amazing star-shaped seed pod from the anise plant has an unusual liquorice flavour and is used in five-spice powder.

Water chestnuts

These are not really chestnuts at all, but walnut-sized bulbs. The crisp white flesh

is enclosed in a brown skin and has a sweet flavour. In the West, they may be bought in cans and are usually rinsed and sliced before adding to savoury dishes.

Won ton skins

Although you can make these yourself, it is easier to buy them ready-made. They are available fresh or frozen in Chinese supermarkets and many delicatessens. Made from wheat flour, egg and water, they are filled with minced savoury mixtures of fish, meat or vegetables, and are then boiled, steamed or fried.

Yellow bean sauce

This thick spicy sauce is sold in jars in most supermarkets, and is made from fermented yellow beans.

Utensils and equipment

In the Chinese kitchen, there are certain essential cooking utensils. If you wish to cook authentic Chinese food yourself at home, it is worth investing in these. They can be purchased in Chinese supermarkets and kitchen shops.

Cleavers: Chinese cooks use these for everything; they are particularly useful for chopping up chicken and ducks.

Steamers: Usually made from bamboo, these come in an assortment of different sizes. The food to be steamed is placed inside and the steamer is then put over a wok or pot of boiling or simmering water. If you are steaming more than one dish, the steamers can often be stacked on top of each other.

Woks: These iron or steel pans have a rounded base to improve heat distribution. The shape means that the heat is spread more evenly over the surface, making it ideal for rapid stir-frying. Woks can be bought in different sizes and are also useful for deep-frying.

SWEETCORN AND CRAB SOUP

Xiaren tang

1 Put the chopped ginger root in a bowl and add the crab meat and sherry. Mix well together and then set aside.

3 Put the stock in a large saucepan and bring to a rolling boil. Add the salt, sweetcorn kernels and the crab and ginger mixture.

2 In a separate bowl, beat the egg white and set aside. Mix the cornflour with the water to make a smooth paste.

1 teaspoon finely chopped ginger root
125g/4oz crab meat
2 teaspoons dry sherry
1 egg white
3 teaspoons cornflour
2 tablespoons cold water
600ml/1 pint clear stock (see page 110)
1 teaspoon salt
125g/4oz sweetcorn kernels
1 spring onion, finely chopped, to garnish

PREPARATION: 10 MINUTES
COOKING: 8-10 MINUTES
SERVES: 4

4 Bring the stock back to the boil, and then add the cornflour paste, stirring constantly. When the soup thickens, stir in the egg white and then serve hot, garnished with shredded spring onion.

BEAN CURD AND PRAWN SOUP

Doufou xiaren tang

1 Put the peeled prawns in a small bowl. In another bowl, break up the egg white with a fork and then add to the prawns and mix well.

2 Cut the ham into small dice, approximately the same size as the peas. Next cut the bean curd into cubes of a similar size.

50g/2oz cooked peeled prawns

1 egg white

50g/2oz cooked ham

125g/4oz bean curd

600ml/1 pint clear stock (see page 110)

50g/2oz peas, fresh or frozen

1 tablespoon soy sauce

1 tablespoon cornflour

salt and freshly ground black pepper

PREPARATION: 10 MINUTES
COOKING: 10-15 MINUTES
SERVES: 4

3 Put the clear stock in a saucepan and bring to the boil. Add the ham, bean curd and peas, and when it starts to bubble again, add the soy sauce and prawns. Boil hard for 15-20 seconds.

4 Mix the cornflour with a little cold water and then pour it into the soup, stirring constantly. When it thickens, season to taste with salt and pepper. Serve immediately.

HOT AND SOUR SOUP

Suan ha tang

| 4 Chinese dried mushrooms |
| 125g/4oz boneless cooked chicken meat, skinned |
| 125g/4oz firm bean curd |
| 75g/3oz bamboo shoots |
| 1 egg |
| salt |
| 600ml/1 pint clear stock (see page 110) |
| 50g/2oz peas, fresh or frozen |
| 2 tablespoons vinegar |
| 1 tablespoon dark soy sauce |
| 2 teaspoons freshly ground black pepper |
| 3 tablespoons cornflour |

1 Put the mushrooms in a bowl, cover with warm water and leave to soak for 20–25 minutes. Drain and reserve the soaking liquid. Squeeze the mushrooms dry and cut into thin shreds. Discard the hard stalks.

3 Pour the stock into a saucepan with the reserved soaking liquid from the mushrooms. Bring to the boil. Add the mushrooms, chicken, bean curd, bamboo shoots, peas and 1 teaspoon of salt. Cook for 2–3 minutes and then add the vinegar, soy sauce and pepper.

2 Thinly shred the chicken, bean curd and bamboo shoots. Break the egg into a bowl, add a pinch of salt and beat lightly together.

4 Mix the cornflour to a smooth paste with 6 tablespoons of cold water. Add to the soup, stirring until it thickens. Add the beaten egg very slowly in a thin, steady stream, pouring it evenly all over the surface of the soup. Serve hot.

PREPARATION:
15 MINUTES + SOAKING TIME
COOKING: 15 MINUTES
SERVES: 4

WON TON SOUP

Wahn tan tang

1 To make the filling for the won tons, put the minced pork in a bowl and add the spinach leaves, salt, sugar and sherry. Mix well together.

2 Put the won ton skins on a lightly floured surface and place one teaspoonful of the pork and spinach filling in the centre of each skin.

3 Bring the opposite corners of each skin together in a fold and pinch the top edges together firmly to seal. Fold the other two corners towards each other and seal.

175g/6oz minced pork
125g/4oz spinach leaves, chopped
1/2 teaspoon salt
1 teaspoon sugar
1 tablespoon sherry
24 won ton skins
900ml/1 1/2 pints clear stock (see page 110)
1 spring onion, finely chopped, to garnish

PREPARATION: 20 MINUTES
COOKING: 7–8 MINUTES
SERVES: 4–6

4 Put the stock in a large saucepan and bring to the boil. Drop in the filled won tons and boil rapidly for 2–3 minutes. Serve immediately, garnished with chopped spring onion.

CRISPY SEAWEED

Cai soong

1 Separate the leaves of the spring greens. Wash them well and then pat dry with absorbent kitchen paper or a clean tea-towel.

2 Using a very sharp knife, shred the spring greens into the thinnest possible shavings. Spread the shavings out on absorbent kitchen paper for about 30 minutes, until thoroughly dry.

| 750g/1½lb spring greens |
| vegetable oil for deep-frying |
| 1½ teaspoons caster sugar |
| 1 teaspoon salt |

3 Heat the oil in a wok or a deep-fat fryer. Turn off the heat for 30 seconds and then add a small batch of spring green shavings. Turn up the heat to moderate and deep-fry the greens until they begin to float on the surface of the oil. Take care as they tend to spit while they are cooking.

4 Remove the greens with a perforated spoon and drain on absorbent kitchen paper. Cook the remaining greens in batches in the same way. When they are all cooked, transfer to a bowl and sprinkle over the sugar and salt. Toss gently to mix and serve warm or cold.

PREPARATION: 10 MINUTES + DRYING TIME
COOKING: 10 MINUTES
SERVES: 8

FIVE-SPICE PORK RIBS

Wuxiang paigu

1kg/2lb pork spare ribs

For the marinade:

1 teaspoon salt

2 tablespoons sugar

2 tablespoons brandy or vodka

2 tablespoons light soy sauce

2 tablespoons hoisin sauce

1 tablespoon dark soy sauce

1 teaspoon five-spice powder

1 teaspoon curry powder (optional)

2 During this time, turn the ribs over once or twice so that they are well covered with the marinade and really absorb the flavours.

1 Cut the pork into individual ribs if this has not been done already by the butcher. Place them in a large ovenproof dish. Mix all the marinade ingredients together and pour over the pork ribs. Leave in a cool place to marinate for 1 hour.

PREPARATION: 5 MINUTES +
MARINATING TIME
COOKING: 40-45 MINUTES
SERVES: 4-6

3 Place the dish in a preheated oven at 200°C/400°F/Gas Mark 6 and cook for 40-45 minutes, turning them once, halfway through cooking. Alternatively, you can remove the ribs from the marinade and cook under a hot grill for 15-20 minutes, turning them occasionally and brushing with marinade, until evenly browned.

4 Chop each rib into 2 or 3 bite-sized pieces with a meat cleaver, if you have one, or serve whole with the sauce poured over them. If you have grilled the ribs, boil up the marinade in a saucepan with a little stock or water to make the sauce.

DEEP-FRIED WON TONS

Cha wahn tan

24 won ton skins

vegetable oil for deep-frying

For the filling:

125g/4oz minced pork

50g/2oz cooked peeled prawns, finely chopped

2 teaspoons finely chopped spring onion

1 tablespoon Chinese rice wine or dry sherry

1 teaspoon sugar

$^{1}/_{2}$ teaspoon salt

For the sauce:

1 tablespoon cornflour

1 tablespoon tomato purée

1 tablespoon sugar

2 tablespoons vinegar

1 tablespoon soy sauce

1 tablespoon vegetable oil

1 Make the filling: put all the filling ingredients in a small bowl and mix thoroughly together to form a smooth mixture.

3 Heat the oil in a deep wok or deep-fat fryer until it is very hot. Turn the heat down and then fry the won tons in batches, for 2-3 minutes or until crispy. Remove and drain on absorbent kitchen paper. Keep warm in a low oven.

2 On a lightly floured surface, put 1 teaspoonful of the filling on each won ton skin. Fold over from corner to corner, wetting a small part of the skin on the sides immediately around the filling. Press them together firmly.

4 Make the sauce: put the cornflour in a bowl and mix to a paste with 4-5 tablespoons of cold water. Stir in the remaining ingredients, except the oil. Heat the oil in a wok or small saucepan and pour in the sauce mixture. Stir over moderate heat for 3-4 minutes until smooth. Serve immediately with the won tons.

PREPARATION: 30 MINUTES
COOKING: 10 MINUTES
SERVES: 4-6

CRAB ROLLS

Xierou jiao

3 Place 2 tablespoons of the filling on half of each wrapping pancake. Fold the other half over and then fold the right side in towards the left, and the left side in towards the right. Roll up tightly and seal with the flour paste.

1 Make the wrapping: sift the flour and salt into a bowl and gradually beat in the water and eggs to form a smooth batter. Place a small, lightly oiled frying pan over moderate heat and pour in 4 tablespoons of batter, rotating it until the base is covered. Cook until the edges curl, then flip over and cook the other side. Cook all the pancakes in this way.

vegetable oil for deep-frying

For the wrapping:

4 tablespoons plain flour

1/2 teaspoon salt

4 tablespoons water

4 eggs, beaten

For the filling:

2 tablespoons oil

1 egg, beaten

1 spring onion, shredded

300g/11oz crab meat, flaked

1 tablespoon dry sherry

salt and freshly ground black pepper

1 tablespoon cornflour

For the flour paste:

1 tablespoon plain flour, mixed with
1 tablespoon water

2 Make the filling: heat the oil in a wok and add the egg, spring onion and crab meat. Stir-fry for a few seconds and then add the sherry, salt and pepper. Dissolve the cornflour in 3 tablespoons of water and add to the pan, stirring until thickened. Remove from the heat and cool.

4 Heat the oil to 180°C/350°F, or until a cube of bread browns in 30 seconds, and deep-fry the crab rolls, a few at a time, until golden brown all over. Drain on absorbent kitchen paper and cut into pieces diagonally. Serve immediately.

PREPARATION: 30 MINUTES
COOKING: 10 MINUTES
SERVES: 6-8

STEAMED CHICKEN DUMPLINGS

Baozi

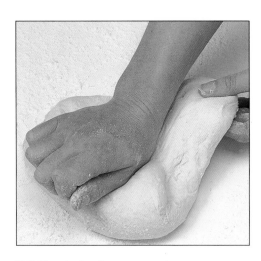

1 Sift the flour into a large mixing bowl and pour in the water. Mix thoroughly to form a stiff dough. Knead for 5 minutes and then place the dough in a bowl, cover with a damp cloth and allow to stand for 10 minutes.

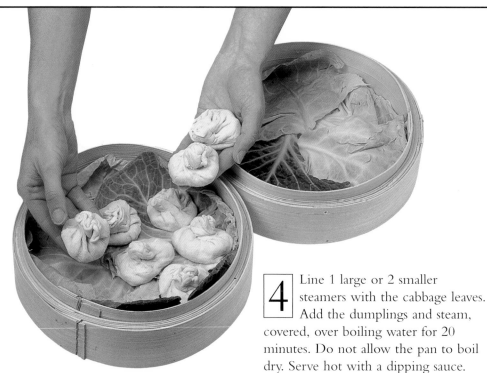

4 Line 1 large or 2 smaller steamers with the cabbage leaves. Add the dumplings and steam, covered, over boiling water for 20 minutes. Do not allow the pan to boil dry. Serve hot with a dipping sauce.

2 Meanwhile, make the filling for the dumplings. Cut the chicken into small bite-sized pieces and place in a bowl with the bamboo shoots, spring onions, ginger, a little salt, the sugar, soy sauce, sherry, stock and sesame oil. Mix well together.

3 Divide the dough in half and form each piece into a 'sausage' shape. Cut each roll into 16 slices and then flatten into rounds. Roll out to circles, about 7.5cm/3 inches in diameter, and place 1 tablespoon of filling in the centre of each. Gather up the edges of the dough around the filling and twist at the top to seal.

| 500g/1lb plain flour |
| 300ml/½ pint water |
| 1 small cabbage, separated into leaves |
| dipping sauce, to serve (see page 111) |
| **For the filling:** |
| 500g/1lb boned chicken breasts, skinned |
| 250g/8oz bamboo shoots, chopped |
| 3 spring onions, finely chopped |
| 3 slices fresh root ginger, peeled and finely chopped |
| salt |
| 2 teaspoons sugar |
| 2 teaspoons light soy sauce |
| 2 tablespoons dry sherry |
| 2 tablespoons clear stock (see page 110) |
| 1 teaspoon sesame oil |

PREPARATION: 45 MINUTES
COOKING: 20 MINUTES
SERVES: 8

SPRING ROLLS

Chun juan

1 Sift the flour and salt into a bowl and beat in the egg and about 300ml/½ pint cold water until you have a smooth batter. Lightly oil a 20cm/8-inch frying pan and set it over moderate heat.

2 Pour in sufficient batter to cover the base of the pan. Cook until the underside is pale golden and then turn the pancake over and cook the other side. Repeat until all the batter is used.

3 Make the filling: heat the oil and then add the pork. Stir-fry for 2-3 minutes until it is evenly browned. Add the garlic and vegetables and stir-fry for 2 minutes. Mix in the prawns and soy sauce, then remove from the heat and allow to cool.

250g/8oz plain flour
pinch of salt
1 egg
1 tablespoon flour, mixed with 1 tablespoon water for the paste
sunflower oil for deep-frying
For the filling:
1 tablespoon sunflower oil
250g/8oz lean pork, shredded
1 garlic clove, crushed
2 celery sticks, sliced
125g/4oz mushrooms, sliced
2 spring onions, chopped
125g/4oz bean sprouts
125g/4oz peeled prawns
2 tablespoons light soy sauce

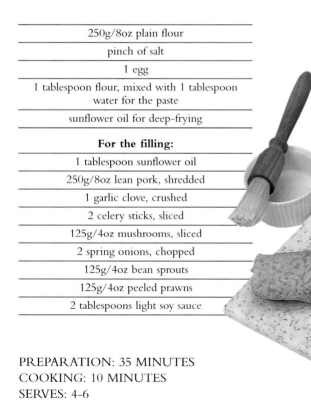

4 Place 2-3 tablespoons of the filling in the centre of each pancake. Fold in the sides and roll up tightly, sealing the edge with a little flour and water paste. Deep-fry the spring rolls in hot oil, two at a time, until evenly golden. Drain and serve hot.

PREPARATION: 35 MINUTES
COOKING: 10 MINUTES
SERVES: 4-6

STEAMED SEA BASS

Qing zheng yu

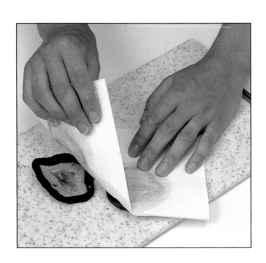

1 Put the mushrooms in a bowl and cover with warm water. Leave to soak for 20 minutes. Squeeze the mushrooms dry and discard the stalks.

2 Slash both sides of the fish diagonally, as deep as the bone, at intervals of about 1cm/½ inch. This prevents the skin from bursting during cooking and allows the heat to penetrate more quickly. Dry the fish and place it on a plate.

3 Thinly shred the fresh ginger root, spring onions, ham, bamboo shoots and mushrooms. Arrange them on top of the sea bass.

2 Chinese dried mushrooms
1 x 450g/1lb sea bass, cleaned and scaled
2 slices fresh ginger root, peeled
2 spring onions
50g/2oz cooked ham
50g/2oz bamboo shoots
3 tablespoons dry sherry
2 tablespoons soy sauce
1 teaspoon sugar
1 teaspoon salt

PREPARATION: 10 MINUTES + SOAKING TIME
COOKING: 15 MINUTES
SERVES: 2

4 Mix together the sherry, soy sauce, sugar and salt, and pour over the fish. Place the fish on the plate in the top of a steamer set over simmering water. Cover and steam vigorously for 15 minutes. Serve hot.

SWEET & SOUR RED-COOKED FISH
Hongshao yu

1 Wash the fish and dry with absorbent kitchen paper. Using a sharp knife, slash both sides of the fish diagonally at 2cm/³/₄-inch intervals. Sprinkle with salt and dredge with flour.

| 1 x 1kg/2lb whole fish, e.g. carp, bream or mullet, cleaned and scaled |
| 1 teaspoon salt |
| 2 tablespoons flour |
| oil for deep-frying |
| 3 tablespoons vegetable oil |
| 15g/¹/₂oz dried Chinese mushrooms, soaked for 20 minutes, drained and stemmed |
| 50g/2oz bamboo shoots, sliced |
| 3 garlic cloves, crushed |
| 4 spring onions, shredded |
| 3 slices fresh ginger root, shredded |
| 25g/1oz water chestnuts, sliced |

For the sweet and sour sauce:

| 1 tablespoon cornflour |
| 2 tablespoons light soy sauce |
| 2 tablespoons sherry |
| 1 tablespoon brown sugar |
| 1 tablespoon vinegar |
| 1 tablespoon tomato purée |
| 4 tablespoons stock |

2 Heat the oil for deep-frying in a wok or deep saucepan and when it is hot, add the fish. Deep-fry for 6-8 minutes, until cooked and crisp. Turn the fish halfway through cooking to cook both sides. Remove and keep warm.

PREPARATION: 15 MINUTES
COOKING: 15 MINUTES
SERVES: 4

3 Heat the vegetable oil in a clean wok or frying pan and add the mushrooms, bamboo shoots, garlic, spring onions, ginger and water chestnuts. Stir-fry briskly for 3-4 minutes.

4 Mix all the sauce ingredients together in a bowl and then stir into the vegetable mixture in the wok. Keep stirring over moderate heat until thickened. Arrange the fish on a serving dish and pour the sauce over the top. Serve immediately.

SQUID AND GREEN PEPPERS

Si chiu chao yau

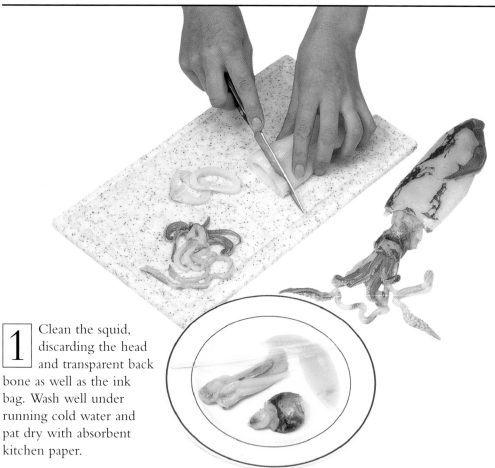

1 Clean the squid, discarding the head and transparent back bone as well as the ink bag. Wash well under running cold water and pat dry with absorbent kitchen paper.

250g/8oz squid

1 green pepper, cored and seeded

2 slices fresh ginger root, peeled

oil for deep-frying

1 teaspoon salt

1 tablespoon soy sauce

1 teaspoon vinegar

freshly ground black pepper

1 teaspoon sesame oil

PREPARATION: 15 MINUTES
COOKING: 5 MINUTES
SERVES: 2-4

2 Peel off the thin skin of the squid and cut the flesh into small pieces – the size of a matchbox. Slice the green pepper and thinly shred the fresh ginger root.

3 Heat the oil in a wok or deep frying pan until it is fairly hot. Deep-fry the prepared squid for about 30 seconds and then remove. Carefully pour off the excess oil, leaving about 1 tablespoon of oil in the pan. Add the ginger, pepper and squid.

4 Stir-fry for a few seconds and then stir in the salt, soy sauce, vinegar and black pepper. Cook for about 1 minute, and then add the sesame oil and serve.

GINGER AND SPRING ONION CRAB
Congjang xieh

1 Break off the legs of the crab and crack the shells into 2 or 3 pieces. Open the shell by laying the crab on its back and pressing down with your thumbs along the suture. Lift out and discard the stomach and intestine and the feathery gills. Crack the shell with a chopper or heavy knife.

1 x 750g/1½lb crab
2 tablespoons sherry
1 tablespoon clear stock (see page 110) or water
2 tablespoons cornflour
4 slices fresh ginger root, peeled
4 spring onions
3 tablespoons oil
1 teaspoon salt
1 tablespoon soy sauce
2 teaspoons sugar

PREPARATION: 20 MINUTES
COOKING: 8-10 MINUTES
SERVES: 2-4

2 Scrape out some of the meat from the shell and place in a bowl with the claws etc. Mix 1 tablespoon of the sherry with the stock or water and cornflour. Pour over the crab and leave to marinate for a few minutes.

3 Finely chop the ginger root and spring onions. In a wok or frying pan, heat the oil until it is very hot. Add the crab meat to the wok and fry briskly for about 1 minute, turning it in the oil.

4 Add the ginger root, spring onions, salt, soy sauce, sugar and the remaining sherry. Cook for about 5 minutes, stirring all the time. Add a little water if the mixture becomes very dry. Serve immediately.

SEAFOOD WITH VEGETABLES

Zhuachao haixian

1 Cut each scallop into 3 or 4 pieces. Peel the prawns and remove the black vein running along the back. Leave whole if small, or cut into 2 or 3 pieces if large. Put the seafood in a bowl with the egg white and half of the cornflour, and mix well.

2 Heat the oil in a deep wok, and then deep-fry the scallops and prawns for 1 minute, stirring all the time to keep the pieces separate. Remove with a perforated spoon and drain on absorbent kitchen paper.

3 Pour off all but 2 tablespoons of oil from the wok. Increase the heat to high and add the vegetables, ginger and spring onions. Stir-fry for about 1 minute. Add the scallops and prawns and stir in the sherry, soy sauce, chilli bean paste (if using) and salt.

4-6 fresh scallops
125-175g/4-6oz headless uncooked prawns
1 egg white
1 tablespoon cornflour
vegetable oil for deep-frying
3 celery sticks, sliced
1 red pepper, seeded and sliced
1-2 carrots, sliced
2 slices fresh ginger root, peeled and shredded
2-3 spring onions, chopped
2 tablespoons sherry
1 tablespoon light soy sauce
2 teaspoons chilli bean paste (optional)
1 teaspoon salt
1 teaspoon sesame oil, to finish

PREPARATION: 20 MINUTES
COOKING: 5 MINUTES
SERVES: 3-4

4 Mix the remaining cornflour to a smooth paste with a little water, and then add to the wok. Stir well until thickened. Sprinkle over the sesame oil and serve immediately.

PRAWNS WITH BROCCOLI

Jielan chao xiaqiu

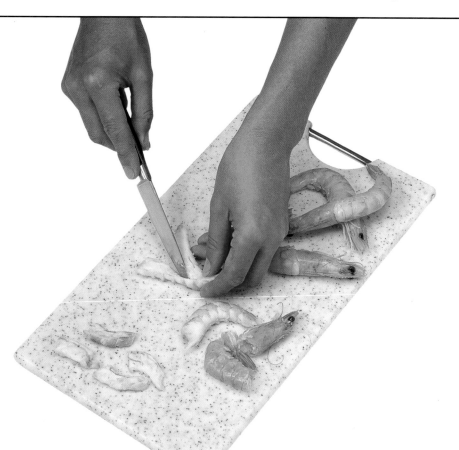

3 Heat 1 tablespoon of the oil in a wok or frying pan and add the prawns. Stir-fry over moderate heat for about 30 seconds. Remove from the wok or pan with a perforated spoon.

1 Wash the prawns, and dry thoroughly on absorbent kitchen paper. Shell the prawns and remove the black intestinal vein. Split each prawn in half lengthways and then cut into small pieces.

250g/8oz cooked king prawns in their shells
1 slice fresh ginger root, peeled and finely chopped
1 tablespoon medium or dry sherry
1 egg white
1 teaspoon cornflour
3 tablespoons vegetable oil
2 spring onions, finely chopped
250g/8oz broccoli, cut into small pieces
1 teaspoon salt

2 Put the prawn pieces in a small bowl with the ginger, sherry, egg white and cornflour. Stir well and then leave in a cool place or the refrigerator to marinate for about 20 minutes.

4 Heat the remaining oil in the wok or pan. Add the spring onions and broccoli and stir well. Add the salt and sugar and stir-fry until the broccoli is just tender. Add the prawns and stir to mix with the broccoli. Serve hot.

PREPARATION: 10 MINUTES +
MARINATING TIME
COOKING: 5 MINUTES
SERVES: 2-3

RAPID-FRIED PRAWNS

Tangcui daxia

3 Pour off all but 1 tablespoon of oil from the wok, and increase the heat to high. Quickly mix together the sauce ingredients and add to the wok with the prawns. Cook for about 1 minute, stirring.

1 Wash and trim the prawns, removing the legs but leaving the tail pieces firmly attached. Remove the black intestinal vein and pat dry with absorbent kitchen paper.

| 500g/1lb headless uncooked prawns |
| vegetable oil for deep-frying |
| 2 teaspoons cornflour |
| **For the sweet and sour sauce:** |
| 2 tablespoon dry sherry |
| 2 tablespoon soy sauce |
| 2 tablespoons vinegar |
| 1 tablespoon sugar |
| 1 teaspoon finely chopped spring onion |
| 1 teaspoon finely chopped fresh ginger root |

2 Heat the oil in a deep wok until it is very hot. Turn down the heat to allow the oil to cool a little, and then deep-fry the prawns until they turn bright pink. Remove them with a perforated spoon and dry on absorbent kitchen paper.

4 Mix the cornflour to a smooth paste with 1 tablespoon cold water. Add to the wok and stir until all the prawns are coated with the sauce.

PREPARATION: 10 MINUTES
COOKING: 5 MINUTES
SERVES: 4

STIR-FRIED PRAWNS

Xiaren chao xiangsu

1 Wash the prawns, removing the heads, shells and legs. Keep the tails intact. Dry thoroughly on absorbent kitchen paper and set aside.

2 Heat the vegetable oil in a deep wok or large frying pan until it starts to smoke. Add the slices of fresh ginger root and fry for 30 seconds to flavour the oil. Remove and discard the ginger.

PREPARATION: 10 MINUTES
COOKING: 8-10 MINUTES
SERVES: 3-4

3 In a bowl, mix together 2 tablespoons of the cornflour with the salt, sherry and egg white. Toss the prawns in this mixture until well coated. Add the prawns to the hot oil and stir-fry until they change colour. Remove with a perforated spoon and set aside.

4 Add the garlic, black beans, mangetout and water chestnuts to the wok and stir-fry for 1-2 minutes. Return the prawns to the wok. Mix the remaining cornflour with the soy sauce and chicken stock and stir into the prawn mixture until thickened. Add the sesame oil and toss well. Serve immediately, garnished with spring onions and coriander sprigs.

500g/1lb large uncooked prawns
4 tablespoons vegetable oil
3 slices fresh ginger root, peeled
2 tablespoons cornflour, plus 1 teaspoon
1 teaspoon salt
1 tablespoon dry sherry
1 egg white
2 garlic cloves, crushed
2 teaspoons black beans, soaked for 1 hour and drained
250g/8oz mangetout, trimmed and cut in half
6 water chestnuts, thinly sliced
1/2 tablespoon soy sauce
2 tablespoons chicken stock
1 teaspoon sesame oil
To garnish:
shredded spring onions
coriander sprigs

PAPER-WRAPPED FISH

Zhibao yu

1 Cut the fish fillets into 2.5cm/ 1-inch squares, about 5mm/¼-inch thick. Place in a bowl and then sprinkle with the salt and sherry. Leave to marinate for 10 minutes.

2 Cut out a 15cm/6-inch square of greaseproof paper for each piece of fish. Brush with oil. Place a piece of fish on each piece of paper and top with some shredded spring onions and ginger.

3 Fold the pieces of paper into envelopes, tucking in the flaps to secure them well. Heat the oil to 180°C/350°F in a wok or deep saucepan.

4 x 125g/4oz fillets of sole or plaice
pinch of salt
2 tablespoons dry sherry
1 tablespoon vegetable oil
2 tablespoons shredded spring onions
2 tablespoons shredded fresh ginger root
vegetable oil for deep-frying
spring onion tassels, to garnish (see page 110)

4 Deep-fry the wrapped fish for 3 minutes, until golden on both sides. Remove carefully with a perforated spoon and drain on absorbent kitchen paper. Arrange on a serving dish garnished with spring onion tassels, if using. The paper wrappings are opened by the guests.

PREPARATION: 15 MINUTES + MARINATING TIME
COOKING: 3 MINUTES
SERVES: 4

SWEET AND SOUR PORK

Kulu rou

1 Cut the pork into 24 small cubes. Cut the bamboo shoots and green pepper into small chunks. Cut the spring onions into 2.5cm/1-inch lengths.

2 Place the pork in a bowl and sprinkle with the salt and brandy. Set aside to marinate for 15 minutes. Add the beaten egg and cornflour and blend well.

PREPARATION: 15 MINUTES +
MARINATING TIME
COOKING: 15 MINUTES
SERVES: 3-4

| 250g/8oz pork |
| 125g/4oz bamboo shoots |
| 1 green pepper, cored and seeded |
| 2 spring onions |
| 1 teaspoon salt |
| 1½ tablespoons brandy |
| 1 egg, beaten |
| 1 tablespoon cornflour |
| oil for deep-frying |
| 3 tablespoons plain flour |
| 425g/14oz can pineapple chunks in juice |
| **For the sauce:** |
| 3 tablespoons vinegar |
| 3 tablespoons sugar |
| ½ teaspoon salt |
| 1 tablespoon tomato purée |
| 1 tablespoon soy sauce |
| 1 tablespoon cornflour |
| 1 teaspoon sesame oil |

3 Heat the oil in a wok or saucepan. Coat each piece of pork with the flour and deep-fry for 3 minutes. Remove the wok from the heat but leave the pork in the oil for a further 2 minutes before removing and draining. Return the wok to the heat and re-fry the meat with the bamboo shoots for 2 minutes. Remove and drain.

4 Pour off the excess oil, leaving 1 tablespoonful in the wok. Add the spring onions and green pepper. Mix the sauce ingredients with a little canned pineapple juice and add to the wok, stirring until thickened. Add the pork, bamboo shoots and pineapple and serve hot.

BARBECUED PORK

Cha shao

1 Trim off any excess fat from the pork and cut the meat into 5 x 5 x 10cm/2 x 2 x 4-inch slices. Mix together all the ingredients for the marinade in a dish.

2 Add the pork to the marinade and leave to marinate for at least 6 hours in the refrigerator. Turn the meat occasionally so that it is well coated with marinade.

1kg/2lb pork shoulder
shredded spring onions, to garnish

For the marinade:

2 tablespoons soy sauce
2 tablespoons dry sherry
2 teaspoons sesame oil
1 teaspoon salt
2 teaspoons ginger juice (squeezed from chopped fresh root ginger)
2 tablespoons clear honey
50g/2oz sugar
2 garlic cloves, crushed

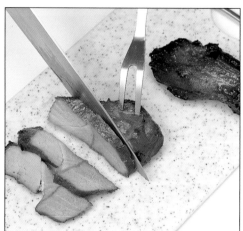

3 Place the pork on a wire rack in a roasting pan. Roast in a preheated oven at 180°C/350°F/Gas Mark 4 for 40-45 minutes, or until tender. Baste the pork frequently with the pan juices.

4 Cut the cooked pork into serving pieces and arrange them on a plate. Garnish with spring onion and serve immediately.

PREPARATION: 10 MINUTES +
MARINATING TIME
COOKING: 40-45 MINUTES
SERVES: 6

PORK IN BLACK BEAN SAUCE

Rousi chao ringjiao

1 Mix together the soy sauce, sherry, sugar and flour in a large bowl. Add the spare ribs, and set aside in a cool place to marinate for 10-15 minutes.

2 Heat the oil in a wok or frying pan and add the spare ribs. Stir-fry for a few minutes until they are golden. Remove with a perforated spoon and drain on absorbent kitchen paper.

3 Add the garlic, spring onions and bean sauce to the wok and stir well. Add the spare ribs with the stock or water, and cook, covered, over high heat for 5 minutes. If necessary, add a little more liquid, replace the lid and cook for a further 5 minutes.

1 tablespoon soy sauce
2 tablespoons dry sherry
1 tablespoon sugar
1 tablespoon plain flour
500g/1lb pork spare ribs, chopped into small pieces
3 tablespoons oil
1 garlic clove, crushed
2 spring onions, sliced diagonally
2 tablespoons crushed black or yellow bean sauce
5 tablespoons clear stock (see page 110) or water
1 small green pepper, seeded and sliced
1 small red pepper, seeded and sliced

4 Add the sliced green and red peppers and stir well. Cook for 2 minutes and then remove from the heat. Serve immediately.

PREPARATION: 10 MINUTES +
MARINATING TIME
COOKING: 15-20 MINUTES
SERVES: 4

RED-COOKED PORK

Hongshao zhuti

1 Put the mushrooms in a bowl and cover with warm water. Set aside to soak for 30 minutes. Squeeze the mushrooms dry and then discard the stems.

2 Put the pork in a large saucepan and cover with cold water. Bring to the boil, then boil for a few minutes and drain. Rinse the pork under running cold water and drain again.

PREPARATION: 15 MINUTES +
SOAKING TIME
COOKING: 2-3 HOURS
SERVES: 4-6

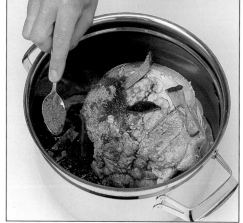

3 Wash the saucepan out and then return the pork to the clean pan. Add the mushrooms, garlic, soy sauce, sherry, sugar and five-spice powder. Cover with a tight-fitting lid and bring to the boil.

4 Lower the heat and simmer very gently for 2-3 hours, turning the pork several times during cooking. There should be very little liquid left at the end of the cooking time. If necessary, increase the heat and simmer, uncovered, until reduced and thickened. Serve garnished with sliced carrot and shredded spring onions.

4 Chinese dried mushrooms
1 x 1.5kg/3lb leg or shoulder of pork
1 garlic clove, crushed
6 tablespoons soy sauce
3 tablespoons dry sherry
3 tablespoons crystallized or brown sugar
1 teaspoon five-spice powder
To garnish:
1 carrot, thinly sliced into rounds
shredded spring onions

RED-OIL DUMPLINGS
Hongyou shuijiao

3 Form the dough into a long sausage, and divide into 5cm/2-inch lengths. Roll each piece into a ball and then roll flat into a small pancake. Place about 1 tablespoon of the filling on each pancake and fold over to form a half-circle. Pinch the edges firmly to seal.

1 Sift the flour into a large bowl. Pour on 150ml/¼ pint boiling water and stir to form a firm dough. Leave for a few minutes and then add 75ml/3 fl oz cold water. Knead well to form a smooth dough.

| 500g/1lb plain flour |
| 500g/1lb minced pork |
| 125g/4oz cooked peeled prawns, finely chopped |
| 1 tablespoon chopped fresh ginger root |
| 1 tablespoon chopped spring onions |
| 1½ teaspoons salt |
| 1 tablespoon soy sauce |
| 1 teaspoon sugar |
| 1 tablespoon water |
| 2 leaves Chinese cabbage, finely chopped |
| pinch of ground pepper |
| 2 teaspoons sesame oil |

For the dipping sauce:

| 1 spring onion, finely chopped |
| 1 garlic clove, finely chopped |
| 2 tablespoons peanut butter |
| 2 teaspoons soy sauce |
| 1 teaspoon red chilli oil |
| 2 teaspoons chicken stock |

2 In a bowl, mix together the pork, prawns, ginger, spring onions, salt, soy sauce, sugar, water, Chinese cabbage, pepper and oil. Beat together to form a paste.

PREPARATION: 25 MINUTES
COOKING: 5-6 MINUTES
SERVES: 6

4 Cook the dumplings in boiling water for 5-6 minutes. Meanwhile, mix together the dipping sauce ingredients. Drain the hot dumplings and serve with the sauce.

PORK AND VEGETABLES

Chop suey

250g/8oz pork fillet

2 tablespoons soy sauce

1 tablespoon dry sherry

2 teaspoons cornflour

2 spring onions

1 slice fresh ginger root, peeled

125g/4oz fresh bean sprouts

5 tablespoons oil

1 small green pepper, cored and seeded

few cauliflower or broccoli florets

2-3 tomatoes, cut into pieces

2 carrots, cut into matchsticks

50g/2oz green beans, trimmed

2 teaspoons salt

1 tablespoon sugar

3 tablespoons clear stock (see page 110) or water

2 Cut the spring onions into 2.5cm/1-inch lengths and finely chop the fresh ginger root. Wash the bean sprouts in a basin of cold water and discard any husks that float to the surface.

3 Heat half of the oil in a wok or heavy frying pan. Stir-fry the sliced pork for 1 minute and then remove with a perforated spoon and put to one side.

1 Cut the pork fillet into small, thin slices. Mix together the soy sauce, sherry and cornflour in a bowl, and add the pork. Stir well until each slice is coated with the mixture.

4 Heat the remaining oil and add the spring onions and ginger root, followed by the rest of the vegetables and the salt and sugar. Stir-fry for 1-2 minutes and then add the sliced pork. Moisten with a little stock or water if wished and stir-fry quickly until the vegetables are tender but still crisp. Serve immediately with rice.

PREPARATION: 15 MINUTES
COOKING: 8-10 MINUTES
SERVES: 3-4

GINGER BEEF WITH PEPPERS

Gungchung si chiu ghao

1 | Put the slices of fillet steak in a bowl and add the soy sauce, 1 teaspoon of the sesame oil, the sliced ginger root, vinegar, water, salt and cornflour. Stir well to mix, until the steak slices are coated thoroughly. Cover and leave in the refrigerator to marinate for at least 20 minutes.

2 | Heat the remaining sesame oil in a wok or frying pan and add the garlic and five-spice powder. Stir-fry for 30 seconds and then add the marinated steak slices. Stir-fry quickly until the meat is browned on the outside yet still pink and tender on the inside. Remove with a perforated spoon and set aside.

3 | Add the chunks of red and green pepper to the wok or frying pan, and stir-fry briskly for 2-3 minutes, tossing them in the oil.

500g/1lb lean fillet steak, thinly sliced
2 teaspoons soy sauce
2 tablespoons sesame oil
2.5cm/1-inch piece fresh ginger root, peeled and sliced
2 teaspoons vinegar
1 tablespoon water
1 teaspoon salt
1 teaspoon cornflour
1 garlic clove, crushed
pinch of five-spice powder
1 red pepper, seeded and cut into chunks
1 green pepper, seeded and cut into chunks
slivers of fresh red chilli, to garnish

4 | Add the strips of steak and any remaining marinade. Stir-fry for 1 minute, until the meat is heated through. Transfer to a serving dish and serve garnished with thin slivers of chilli.

PREPARATION: 10 MINUTES
+ MARINATING TIME
COOKING: 5 MINUTES
SERVES: 3-4

BEEF WITH CASHEW NUTS

Yeu gua chao ghao

1 Cut the fillet steak into thin slices, removing any fat. Place in a bowl and add the soy sauce, sherry, 2 teaspoons of the sesame oil, the water, cornflour, seasoning and ginger. Cover and leave in the refrigerator to marinate for at least 20 minutes.

2 Heat the remaining sesame oil in a deep wok or heavy frying pan. Remove the strips of steak from the marinade and stir-fry quickly in the hot oil for 2 minutes, until brown and sealed on the outside. Remove and set aside. Reserve the marinade.

3 Add the garlic, cashew nuts and celery to the wok or frying pan, and then stir-fry quickly over moderate heat for 2–3 minutes, tossing well.

500g/1lb lean fillet steak
2 tablespoons soy sauce
1 tablespoon dry sherry
3 tablespoons sesame oil
3 tablespoons water
2 teaspoons cornflour
salt and freshly ground black pepper
1 tablespoon finely chopped peeled fresh ginger root
2 garlic cloves, crushed
125g/4oz unsalted roasted cashew nuts
3 celery sticks, sliced diagonally

4 Return the steak to the wok with the reserved marinade and mix well with the nuts and celery. Increase the heat and continue cooking, stirring all the time, until the sauce thickens. Transfer to a serving dish.

PREPARATION: 10 MINUTES + MARINATING
COOKING: 8 MINUTES
SERVES: 3–4

BEEF IN OYSTER SAUCE

Hao yiu niu jou

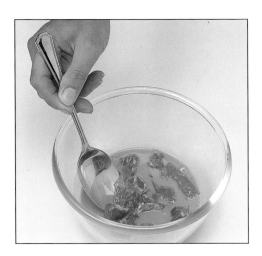

1 Cut the beef into thickish slices, about the size of a matchbox. In a bowl, mix together the oyster sauce, sherry and cornflour, and marinate the beef in this mixture for about 20 minutes.

2 Cut the broccoli into small florets. Slice the bamboo shoots and carrot into slices, about the same size as the beef slices. If using Chinese dried mushrooms, soak them in warm water for 20 minutes, squeeze dry, discard the stalks and finely slice the mushrooms.

250g/8oz beef steak
2 tablespoons oyster sauce
1 tablespoon dry sherry
1 tablespoon cornflour
125g/4oz broccoli
125g/4oz bamboo shoots
1 carrot, peeled
125g/4oz button mushrooms or 3-4 Chinese dried mushrooms
4 tablespoons oil
2 slices fresh ginger root, peeled and chopped
2 spring onions, chopped
1 teaspoon salt
1 teaspoon sugar
2 tablespoons clear stock (see page 110) or water

PREPARATION: 15 MINUTES +
MARINATING TIME
COOKING: 5 MINUTES
SERVES: 4

3 Heat half of the oil in a wok or heavy frying pan. Add the beef and stir-fry for 10-15 seconds. Remove with a perforated spoon and set aside.

4 Heat the remaining oil and then add the ginger root and spring onions, followed by all the vegetables. Add the salt and sugar and stir-fry for 1½ minutes. Add the beef, stir well and moisten with a little stock or water. Heat through and serve immediately.

ROAST PEKING DUCK

Beijing kao ya

1 Wash the duck and pat dry with absorbent kitchen paper. Dissolve the sugar and salt in the water and rub all over the duck. Leave for several hours in a cool place until dry. Place the duck in a roasting pan and cook in a preheated oven at 200°C/400°F/Gas Mark 6 for 1 hour.

2 Prepare the vegetables for serving with the duck. Make spring onion flowers by making several cuts from top to bottom along each spring onion, without cutting through the base. Leave in a bowl of iced water to open. Cut the leeks and cucumber into 7.5cm/3-inch strips and arrange on a dish with the spring onions.

3 Just before the duck is ready, make the sauce. Put all the ingredients in a small saucepan and heat gently over low heat for 2-3 minutes, stirring constantly. Pour the sauce into a small serving bowl.

1 x 1.5-1.75kg/3-4¼lb duckling
1 tablespoon sugar
1 teaspoon salt
300ml/½ pint water
For the sauce:
3 tablespoons yellow bean sauce
2 tablespoons sugar
1 tablespoon sesame oil
To serve:
12 spring onions
4 leeks
½ cucumber
24 Mandarin Pancakes (see page 110)

PREPARATION: 25 MINUTES +
STANDING TIME
COOKING: 1 HOUR
SERVES: 4-6

4 Put the roasted duck on a serving dish and tear the meat off the bones with a fork, or, alternatively, carve it into neat slices. Serve with the Mandarin Pancakes and sauce. Each person helps themselves – spread a little sauce on each pancake, place a little leek and cucumber in the middle plus some duck, and then roll up.

SHREDDED CHICKEN AND CELERY

Yuxiang jisi

1 Cut the chicken breast meat into shreds and place in a bowl. Add the salt, egg white and cornflour and mix well. Cut the celery, green pepper, ginger root and spring onions into slivers, the same size as the chicken shreds.

2 Heat the oil in a wok or heavy frying pan and add the chicken shreds. Stir-fry over moderate heat until the chicken is lightly and evenly coloured. Remove the chicken with a perforated spoon and set aside.

3 Increase the heat and, when the oil is very hot, add the ginger root and spring onions followed by the celery and green pepper. Stir-fry for about 30 seconds over high heat.

250g/8oz chicken breast meat, boned and skinned

½ teaspoon salt

1 egg white

1 tablespoon cornflour

1 small celery stick

1 green pepper, cored and seeded

4 slices fresh ginger root, peeled

2 spring onions

4 tablespoons oil

2 tablespoons soy sauce

1 tablespoon dry sherry

4 Return the chicken shreds to the wok with the soy sauce and sherry. Mix well and cook for a further 1–1½ minutes, stirring all the time. Transfer to a serving dish and serve immediately.

PREPARATION: 15 MINUTES
COOKING: 7-8 MINUTES
SERVES: 3-4

CHICKEN WITH WALNUTS
Kung bao jiding

1 Cut the chicken flesh into small cubes, about the size of sugar lumps. Place them in a bowl with the salt, and then mix in the egg white. Finally, mix in 1 tablespoon of the cornflour.

2 Heat the oil in a wok or heavy frying pan and, when it is hot, add the chicken cubes. Stir-fry them briskly for a few minutes until the colour changes from pink to white. Remove them from the wok with a perforated spoon and set aside.

3 Add the spring onions, ginger, chillies and walnuts to the hot oil in the wok, and then stir in the bean sauce. Stir a few times and then add the green pepper. Return the chicken to the wok and stir well. Add the sugar and sherry, and stir-fry for about 1 minute.

275g–350g/10–12oz boneless chicken breasts, skinned
½ teaspoon salt
1 egg white
1 tablespoon cornflour, plus 1 teaspoon
4 tablespoons vegetable oil
2 spring onions, cut into 1cm/½-inch lengths
2 slices fresh ginger root, peeled
3–4 dried red chillies, thinly sliced
50g/2oz shelled walnuts, roughly chopped
1 tablespoon yellow or black bean sauce
1 green pepper, seeded and cut into chunks
1 teaspoon sugar
2 tablespoons dry sherry

4 Mix the remaining teaspoon of cornflour to a smooth paste with 1 tablespoon of cold water. Add this mixture to the wok and blend well until thickened. Transfer to a warm serving dish and serve immediately.

PREPARATION: 15 MINUTES
COOKING: 5 MINUTES
SERVES: 3-4

STIR-FRIED SESAME CHICKEN
Mala jiding

1 Toss the chicken cubes in the cornflour until they are evenly coated. Heat the oil in a wok or frying pan and, when hot, add the chicken pieces. Stir-fry over high heat for 45 seconds and then remove from the wok with a perforated spoon. Set aside.

3 Add the lard to the wok and, when it has melted, add the remaining soy sauce, the sesame seed paste, sesame oil, stock or water, chilli sauce and sherry. Mix well together and cook for 1 minute.

2 Add the green pepper to the hot oil in the wok, and stir-fry briskly over moderate heat for 1 minute. Stir in 1 tablespoon of the soy sauce and then remove the green pepper with a perforated spoon and set aside.

500g/1lb boned chicken breasts, cut into 2.5cm/1-inch cubes
1½ teaspoons cornflour
3½ tablespoons oil
1 green pepper, seeded and cut into 2.5cm/1-inch pieces
2½ tablespoons soy sauce
15g/½oz lard
2½ tablespoons sesame seed paste
1 tablespoon sesame oil
1 tablespoon stock or water
1 teaspoon chilli sauce
1 tablespoon dry sherry
sesame seeds, to garnish

PREPARATION: 10 MINUTES
COOKING: 7-8 MINUTES
SERVES: 3-4

4 Return the chicken cubes to the sauce mixture in the wok, and stir over high heat for about 45 seconds. Mix in the reserved green pepper. Cook for a further 30 seconds until the pepper is just tender. Transfer to a serving dish and serve immediately, garnished with sesame seeds.

FRIED EIGHT-PIECE CHICKEN
Shao ba kuai

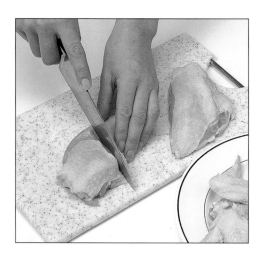

1 Wash the chicken inside and out, and then pat dry with absorbent kitchen paper. Carefully cut off the legs, wings and breasts from the chicken, and then cut each breast in half.

3 Remove the chicken from the marinade and coat each piece with cornflour. Reserve any leftover marinade. Meanwhile, heat the lard in a wok or large frying pan.

2 In a large bowl, mix together the spring onions and fresh ginger root with 1 tablespoon of the sherry, 1 teaspoon of the sugar and 1 tablespoon of the soy sauce. Add the chicken pieces and turn in the marinade until well coated. Leave to marinate for about 5 minutes.

1 x 1.25kg/2¹/₂lb spring chicken
2–3 spring onions, finely chopped
2–3 slices fresh ginger root, finely chopped
2 tablespoons dry sherry
1 tablespoon sugar
3 tablespoons soy sauce
3 tablespoons cornflour
125g/4oz lard
1 teaspoon sesame oil
chopped chives, to garnish

PREPARATION: 20 MINUTES
COOKING: 15 MINUTES
SERVES: 4

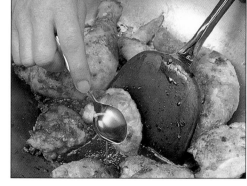

4 Add the chicken to the wok and fry over moderate heat until golden brown all over and cooked through. Pour off the excess lard and add the remaining sherry, sugar, soy sauce and leftover marinade. Bring to the boil, stirring. Stir in the sesame oil and then serve the chicken pieces immediately, garnished with chives.

NOODLES WITH CRAB SAUCE

Congjang mian

1 Fill a large saucepan with salted water and bring it to the boil. Throw in the egg noodles and boil rapidly for 5 minutes, or until they are just tender but still firm.

2 Drain the cooked noodles in a colander and when they are thoroughly dry, transfer them to a warmed serving dish. Set aside in a warm place while you prepare the sauce.

PREPARATION: 10 MINUTES
COOKING: 15 MINUTES
SERVES: 2-3

3 Wash the spinach or cabbage leaves thoroughly and then drain and pat dry with absorbent kitchen paper. Cut into rough pieces. Heat the oil in a wok or heavy frying pan and add the crab meat and spinach or cabbage. Stir-fry for 1 minute.

pinch of salt
150g/5oz egg noodles
125g/4oz spinach or cabbage
2 tablespoons oil
125g/4oz drained canned crab meat
1 teaspoon soy sauce
250ml/8 fl oz clear stock (see page 110)
1 spring onion, finely chopped, to garnish

4 Add the soy sauce and stock to the wok and cook briskly for 2-3 minutes, stirring occasionally. Pour the crab meat sauce over the warm egg noodles and sprinkle with chopped spring onion to garnish. Serve immediately.

NOODLES IN SOUP

Tang mian

1 Put the prawns in a bowl with a pinch of salt. Mix the cornflour to a smooth paste with 1 tablespoon cold water, and then stir into the prawns. Thinly shred the bamboo shoots or mushrooms, and the spinach or Chinese leaves.

2 Fill a large saucepan with salted water and bring to the boil. Add the egg noodles and boil until just tender. Drain well and place the noodles in a large warmed serving bowl or 4 individual bowls. Bring the stock to the boil and pour over the noodles with half of the soy sauce. Keep warm.

4 Stir a few times, and then add 1½ teaspoons salt, the remaining soy sauce and the sherry. Cook for 1–2 minutes, stirring constantly. Pour the mixture over the noodles and sprinkle with sesame oil. Serve hot.

250g/8oz cooked peeled prawns
salt
1 teaspoon cornflour
125g/4oz bamboo shoots or button mushrooms
125g/4oz spinach leaves or Chinese leaves
375g/12oz egg noodles
600ml/1 pint chicken stock
2 tablespoons light soy sauce
3 tablespoons vegetable oil
2 spring onions, thinly shredded
2 tablespoons dry sherry
1–2 teaspoons sesame oil, to finish

3 Heat the oil in a wok or frying pan and add the shredded spring onions to flavour the oil. Add the prawn mixture and the shredded bamboo shoots or mushrooms and spinach or Chinese leaves.

PREPARATION: 15 MINUTES
COOKING: 15 MINUTES
SERVES: 4

CHOW MEIN FRIED NOODLES
Chao mian

1 Fill a large saucepan with salted water and bring to the boil. Add the egg noodles and cook until tender but still firm. Drain in a colander and rinse under cold running water until cool. Set aside.

3 Heat the remaining oil in the wok and add the spring onions and drained noodles, with about half of the stir-fried meat and vegetable mixture.

2 Heat about 3 tablespoons of the oil in a hot wok or frying pan. Add the onion, shredded meat, mange-tout and bean sprouts, and stir-fry for 1 minute. Add 1 teaspoon of salt and stir a few more times. Remove from the wok with a perforated spoon and keep warm.

PREPARATION: 15 MINUTES
COOKING: 10 MINUTES
SERVES: 3-4

500g/1lb egg noodles
salt
4 tablespoons vegetable oil
1 onion, thinly sliced
125g/4oz cooked meat, e.g. pork, chicken or ham, shredded
125g/4oz mangetout, trimmed
125g/4oz fresh bean sprouts
2-3 spring onions, thinly shredded
2 tablespoons light soy sauce
1 tablespoon sesame oil or chilli sauce, to finish

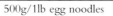

4 Mix in the soy sauce and stir-fry for 1-2 minutes, or until heated through. Transfer the mixture to a warmed serving dish and pour the remaining stir-fried meat and vegetable mixture over the top. Sprinkle with sesame oil or chilli sauce and serve immediately.

SICHUAN NOODLES

Dan dan mian

1 Bring a large saucepan of salted water to the boil. Add the thin egg noodles and cook, according to the packet instructions, until tender. Drain well and divide between 4 individual bowls or one large one.

2 Put the minced pork in a bowl with the soy sauce, sherry and ½ teaspoon salt. Mix well to coat the pork. Heat the oil in a deep wok or frying pan, and add the pork. Stir-fry until lightly browned. Remove with a perforated spoon and dry on absorbent kitchen paper.

3 Add the garlic, ginger, spring onions and chillies to the wok and stir-fry for 1 minute. Add the hot soy bean paste and peanut butter, and stir well over moderate heat for a few seconds.

4 Add the chicken stock, bring to the boil and then simmer for about 5 minutes, until thickened. Stir in the pork and continue cooking over low heat for 1 minute. Ladle the sauce over the noodles and sprinkle with plenty of pepper. Garnish with chilli.

salt
375g/12oz thin egg noodles
250g/8oz minced pork
2 tablespoons dark soy sauce
1 tablespoon dry sherry
4 tablespoons groundnut or vegetable oil
3 garlic cloves, crushed
2.5cm/1-inch piece fresh ginger root, peeled and finely chopped
3 spring onions, chopped
1-2 fresh red chillies, seeded and finely chopped
1 tablespoon hot soy bean paste
1 tablespoon peanut butter
175ml/6 fl oz chicken stock
freshly ground black pepper
chopped fresh red chilli, to garnish

PREPARATION: 15 MINUTES
COOKING: 10 MINUTES
SERVES: 4

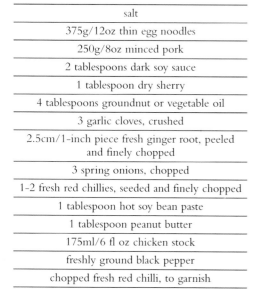

NOODLES WITH SHRIMP SAUCE

Lu mein

salt

500g/1lb egg noodles

75g/3oz dried Chinese mushrooms

2 tablespoons vegetable oil

175g/6oz boned, skinned chicken, diced

1 garlic clove, crushed

2 slices fresh ginger root, peeled and chopped

4 spring onions, cut diagonally into
1 cm/½-inch pieces

175g/6oz shelled prawns

2 tablespoons soy sauce

2 tablespoons dry sherry

900ml/1½ pints clear stock (see page 110)

2 tablespoons cornflour

50g/2oz cooked lean ham, shredded

3 Heat the oil in a deep wok or large saucepan. Add the chicken, garlic and ginger, and stir-fry for 2-3 minutes. Add the spring onions and Chinese mushrooms and stir-fry for 2 minutes.

1 Bring a large saucepan of salted water to the boil and add the egg noodles. Boil rapidly according to package instructions until they are just tender. Drain and divide the noodles between 6 serving dishes. Keep warm.

2 While the noodles are cooking, place the dried Chinese mushrooms in a bowl, cover with warm water and leave to soak for 20 minutes. Drain, reserving the soaking liquid. Discard the stalks and slice the caps thinly.

4 Add the prawns, soy sauce, sherry, ½ teaspoon salt and the clear stock. Bring to the boil and then simmer over gentle heat for 5 minutes. Mix the cornflour with a little water and stir into the liquid in the wok. Keep stirring over low heat until it thickens slightly. Pour over the noodles, sprinkle with the shredded ham and serve immediately.

PREPARATION: 10 MINUTES +
SOAKING TIME
COOKING: 20 MINUTES
SERVES: 6

STEAMED MEAT DUMPLINGS

Shao bao

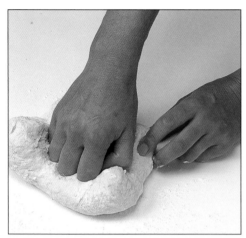

1 Sift the flour and baking powder into a mixing bowl. Mix in the water and knead well to make a smooth dough. Cover the bowl with a damp cloth and place a small plate on top. Leave the dough to rise at room temperature for 2 hours.

2 Meanwhile, make the filling: mince the pork and place in a bowl with the sherry, soy sauce, sugar, salt, sesame oil, ginger and cornflour. Mix well together to coat the meat thoroughly.

3 Divide the dough in half, place on a lightly floured surface and knead well. Shape each half into a long sausage-like roll, 5cm/2 inches in diameter. Slice each roll into about 15 rounds. Flatten each round with the palm of your hand and then with a rolling pin. Roll out into pancakes, about 7.5cm/3 inches in diameter.

500g/1lb plain flour
4 teaspoons baking powder
250ml/8 fl oz water
Spicy Dipping Sauce, to serve (see page 111)
For the filling:
500g/1lb pork (not too lean)
1 tablespoon sherry
3 tablespoons soy sauce
2 teaspoons sugar
1 teaspoon salt
1 tablespoon sesame oil
2 teaspoons finely chopped peeled fresh ginger root
1 teaspoon cornflour

PREPARATION: 30 MINUTES +
RISING TIME
COOKING: 20 MINUTES
SERVES: 6

4 Place a little of the filling in the centre of each pancake, and gather the sides of the dough up around the filling to meet at the top. Twist the top to close tightly. Arrange the dumplings in a muslin-lined steamer, cover and steam vigorously for 20 minutes. Serve hot with the Spicy Dipping Sauce.

SPECIAL EGG-FRIED RICE

Chao fan

1 Break the eggs into a small bowl and add 1 teaspoon of the finely chopped spring onions and a pinch of the salt. Beat lightly together with a fork to combine them.

2 Heat about 1 tablespoon of the oil in a hot wok or heavy frying pan and add the beaten egg mixture. Stir constantly until the eggs are scrambled and set. Remove the scrambled eggs from the wok and set aside in a bowl.

3 Heat the remaining oil in the wok, and add the prawns, meat, bamboo shoots, peas and the remaining chopped spring onions. Stir-fry briskly for 1 minute, and then stir in the soy sauce.

2-3 eggs
2 spring onions, finely chopped
2 teaspoons salt
3 tablespoons vegetable oil
125g/4oz cooked peeled prawns
125g/4oz cooked meat, e.g. chicken or pork, diced
50g/2oz bamboo shoots, diced
4 tablespoons fresh or frozen peas, cooked
1 tablespoon light soy sauce
375-500g/12oz-1lb cold cooked rice
chopped spring onions, to garnish

4 Stir-fry for 2-3 minutes and then add the cooked rice, together with the scrambled eggs and the remaining salt. Stir well to break up the scrambled eggs into small pieces and separate the grains of rice. Serve hot, garnished with spring onions.

PREPARATION: 10 MINUTES
COOKING: 8-10 MINUTES
SERVES: 4

AUBERGINES IN FRAGRANT SAUCE

Qiezi Sichuan

1 Remove the peel from the aubergines, and cut the flesh into strips about the size of potato chips. Cut the pork into thin shreds, the size of matchsticks. Chop the spring onions, ginger root and garlic.

2 Heat the oil for deep-frying in a deep wok or saucepan. When it is hot, add the aubergine 'chips' and deep-fry for 1-2 minutes, until golden. Remove with a perforated spoon and drain on absorbent kitchen paper.

PREPARATION: 15 MINUTES
COOKING: 5-7 MINUTES
SERVES: 2-3

3 Carefully pour off the oil to leave only 1 tablespoonful in the wok or pan. Quickly stir-fry the spring onions, ginger and garlic, followed by the pork. Blend in the soy sauce, sherry and chilli sauce, and then add the aubergine 'chips'. Stir-fry for 1-2 minutes.

| 250g/8oz aubergines |
| 125g/4oz pork fillet |
| 2 spring onions |
| 1 slice fresh ginger root, peeled |
| 1 garlic clove, peeled |
| oil for deep-frying |
| 1 tablespoon soy sauce |
| 1 tablespoon dry sherry |
| 2 teaspoons chilli sauce |
| 2 tablespoons cornflour |

4 Mix the cornflour with a little water in a small bowl and then stir it into the aubergine mixture in the wok or pan. When the sauce thickens, remove from the heat and serve immediately.

STIR-FRIED VEGETABLES

Zhi wu si bao

1 Cover the dried mushrooms with warm water, cover and leave to soak for 25–30 minutes. Drain them and squeeze dry. Discard the hard stalks and slice the mushrooms thinly. If using fresh mushrooms, just wash and slice them.

2 Cut the Chinese leaves and carrots diagonally into thin slices. If the French beans are small, leave them whole. However, if they are long, cut them in half.

PREPARATION: 10 MINUTES +
SOAKING TIME
COOKING: 3–4 MINUTES
SERVES: 3–4

3 Heat the oil in a hot wok or heavy frying pan until it is smoking. Reduce the heat and add the Chinese leaves and carrots. Stir-fry them briskly for 30 seconds.

5–6 Chinese dried mushrooms or 50g/2oz button mushrooms
250g/8oz Chinese leaves
175g/6oz carrots, peeled
125g/4oz French beans, trimmed
4 tablespoons vegetable oil
1 teaspoon salt
1 teaspoon sugar
1 tablespoon light soy sauce

4 Add the beans and mushrooms and continue stir-frying for 30 seconds. Add the salt and sugar and toss and turn the vegetables until well blended. Stir in the soy sauce and cook for 1 more minute. Transfer to a warmed serving dish and serve immediately.

CHINESE BRAISED VEGETABLES

Su shijin

5-6 Chinese dried mushrooms
250g/8oz firm bean curd
salt
4 tablespoons vegetable oil
125g/4oz carrots, sliced
125g/4oz mangetout, trimmed
125g/4oz Chinese leaves, shredded
2 spring onions, cut into 1.25cm/¹/₂-inch lengths
125g/4oz bamboo shoots, sliced
1 teaspoon sugar
1 tablespoon light soy sauce
1 teaspoon cornflour
1 teaspoon sesame oil

3 Heat about half of the oil in a heavy-based saucepan. Add the bean curd pieces and fry until lightly browned on both sides. Remove the bean curd, and then heat the remaining oil in the pan. Add the vegetables and stir-fry for 2 minutes. Stir in the bean curd with 1 teaspoon salt, the sugar and soy sauce. Cover, reduce the heat and braise for 3 minutes.

1 Put the Chinese dried mushrooms in a bowl and cover with warm water. Set aside to soak for 25-30 minutes, and then drain well. Discard the hard stalks, and cut the mushroom caps into thin slices.

PREPARATION: 20 MINUTES +
SOAKING TIME
COOKING: 15 MINUTES
SERVES: 4

2 Cut each cake of bean curd into 12 small pieces. Bring a saucepan of lightly salted water to the boil and add the bean curd. Boil for 2-3 minutes until firm. Remove the bean curd pieces with a perforated spoon and drain well on absorbent kitchen paper.

4 Meanwhile, mix the cornflour to a smooth paste with 1 tablespoon cold water. Stir into the braised vegetables in the pan. Increase the heat and continue stirring until the sauce thickens. Sprinkle in the sesame oil and serve immediately.

STIR-FRIED GREEN BEANS
Chao doujiao

1 Top and tail the green beans and then remove the 'strings' along the sides. Break the beans into 5cm/ 2-inch lengths. It does not matter if they are thin or thick beans.

3 Add the green beans and cashew nuts to the wok and toss well to combine with the other vegetables and spices. Stir-fry quickly for 1 minute to brown the cashew nuts.

500g/1lb green beans
3 tablespoons oil
2 garlic cloves, crushed
2 shallots, thinly sliced
1 slice fresh ginger root, peeled and chopped
1 fresh red chilli, seeded and finely chopped
1/2 teaspoon salt
50g/2oz unsalted cashew nuts
125ml/4 fl oz chicken stock
2 tablespoons sherry
1 tablespoon light soy sauce
1 teaspoon vinegar
1 teaspoon sugar
freshly ground black pepper

2 Heat the oil in a deep wok or large frying pan. Add the garlic, shallots and fresh ginger root. Stir-fry briskly over moderate heat for 1 minute. Stir in the chilli and salt and continue stir-frying for 30 seconds.

PREPARATION: 10 MINUTES
COOKING: 7-8 MINUTES
SERVES: 4

4 Add the chicken stock, sherry, soy sauce, vinegar and sugar to the wok and bring to the boil. Reduce the heat slightly and continue stir-frying for about 4 minutes, until the beans are cooked and the liquid has thickened. Serve immediately sprinkled with plenty of ground black pepper.

STIR-FRIED MUSHROOMS

Donggu ch'ao

1 Put the dried shiitake mushrooms in a bowl and cover with boiling water. Leave them to soak for 15 minutes. Drain well and discard the hard stalks.

3 Add the dried mushrooms and button mushrooms to the wok or pan and cook for 5 minutes, stirring all the time.

50g/2oz dried shiitake mushrooms, sliced
1 tablespoon oil
1 teaspoon finely chopped fresh ginger root
2 spring onions, finely chopped
1 garlic clove, crushed
250g/8oz button mushrooms
1 x 227g/8oz can straw mushrooms, drained
1 teaspoon chilli bean sauce or chilli powder
2 teaspoons dry sherry
2 teaspoons dark soy sauce
1 tablespoon chicken stock
pinch of sugar
pinch of salt
1 teaspoon sesame oil

2 Heat the oil in a wok or deep frying pan over moderate heat. Add the fresh ginger root, spring onions and garlic and stir-fry briskly for 5–10 seconds.

4 Add the straw mushrooms, chilli bean sauce or chilli powder, sherry, soy sauce, chicken stock, sugar, salt and sesame oil. Mix well and then stir-fry for 5 more minutes. Transfer to a warmed serving dish and serve.

PREPARATION: 5 MINUTES +
SOAKING TIME
COOKING: 10 MINUTES
SERVES: 4

SPICY VEGETABLES

Chao chop choi

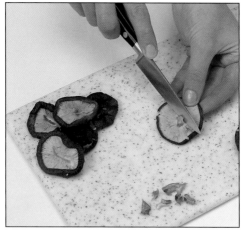

1 Put the water in a large saucepan and bring to the boil. Add the cellophane noodles to the pan, bring back to the boil and boil rapidly for 3 minutes. Drain the noodles well and set aside.

2 Put the dried shiitake mushrooms in a bowl and cover with boiling water. Leave them to soak for 20 minutes and then drain the mushrooms. Discard the hard stalks and reserve the caps.

3 Heat 2 tablespoons of the oil in a deep wok or frying pan, and add the cabbage and salt. Stir-fry for 2 minutes, and then remove. Heat the remaining oil in the wok or pan and stir-fry the carrot for 1 minute. Add the cabbage with the spinach and mushrooms and stir-fry for 2 minutes.

1.2 litres/2 pints water
200g/7oz transparent cellophane noodles
8 dried shiitake mushrooms
3 tablespoons sunflower oil
250g/8oz Chinese cabbage or Chinese leaves, shredded
pinch of salt
1 large carrot, thinly sliced
125g/4oz fresh spinach, cooked and chopped
For the sauce:
1 tablespoon sesame oil
1 tablespoon soy sauce
2 teaspoons sugar
2 teaspoons sesame seeds
1/2 teaspoon salt

PREPARATION: 10 MINUTES + SOAKING TIME
COOKING: 15 MINUTES
SERVES: 4

4 Make the sauce: put all the ingredients in a pan over moderate heat and stir well. Bring to the boil and then pour over the vegetables in the wok. Add the cellophane noodles and toss well until thoroughly combined. Heat through and serve immediately.

LYCHEE SORBET

Lichi bian choz ling

| 1 x 500g/1lb can of lychees |
| 125g/4oz granulated sugar |
| 2 tablespoons lemon or lime juice |
| 2 egg whites |
| thinly pared rind of 1 lime, to decorate |

1 Drain the juice from the lychees into a measuring jug and make up to 300ml/½ pint with cold water. Pour into a saucepan and stir in the sugar. Heat gently, stirring, until the sugar has dissolved. Bring to the boil, then simmer gently for 10 minutes. Remove from the heat and allow to cool slightly.

2 Purée the lychees in a blender or food processor or press through a sieve. Mix with the sugar syrup and lemon or lime juice. Pour the mixture into a shallow freezer container and place in the freezer for 1-2 hours, until nearly frozen.

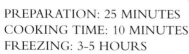

PREPARATION: 25 MINUTES
COOKING TIME: 10 MINUTES
FREEZING: 3-5 HOURS
SERVES: 6

3 Whisk the egg whites in a clean, dry bowl until fairly stiff. Cut the frozen lychee mixture into small pieces and then work in a blender or food processor to break down the crystals. Transfer to a bowl and quickly fold in the whisked egg white. Pour into a freezer container and freeze for 2-3 hours, until firm.

4 Plunge the pared lime rind into a saucepan of boiling water and blanch for 2 minutes. Drain, refresh and pat dry. Cut into thin strips and serve sprinkled over the sorbet.

FRUIT FRITTERS

Basi shuiguo

1 Peel and core the apples and then cut each one into 8 pieces. Peel the bananas and cut each one in half lengthways. Cut each half into 3-4 sections.

2 Make a batter: beat the egg in a small bowl and then blend in the cornflour and sufficient cold water to make a smooth batter. Dip each piece of fruit into the batter.

3 Heat the oil for deep-frying in a deep wok or heavy saucepan, and when it is hot add the pieces of fruit in batter, a few at a time. Deep-fry for 2-3 minutes, until crisp and golden. Remove with a perforated spoon and drain on absorbent kitchen paper.

2 large, firm eating apples
2 bananas
1 egg
4 tablespoons cornflour
vegetable oil for deep-frying
125g/4oz sugar
3 tablespoons sesame oil
1 tablespoon sesame seeds
To serve:
fresh lime slices
banana slices

4 Heat the sugar and sesame oil over low heat for 5 minutes. Add 3 tablespoons of water and stir for 2 minutes. Add the fruit fritters and sesame seeds and stir slowly, until each fritter is coated with syrup. As soon as the syrup caramelizes, remove the fritters and plunge into a bowl of cold water to harden the 'toffee'. Serve with sliced lime and banana.

PREPARATION: 10 MINUTES
COOKING: 15-20 MINUTES
SERVES: 6-8

EIGHT-JEWEL RICE PUDDING

Babao fan

250g/8oz glutinous rice
40g/1½oz lard
2 tablespoons sugar
30 raisins
10 walnut halves, chopped
1 x 250g/8oz can of sweetened chestnut purée
4 glacé cherries, sliced in half
4 pieces candied angelica
12 dried red dates, stoned
For the syrup:
3 tablespoons sugar
300ml/½ pint cold water
1 tablespoon cornflour

1 Put the rice in a saucepan, cover with water and bring to the boil. Reduce the heat, cover tightly and cook for 10-15 minutes, or until the water is absorbed. Add 25g/1oz of the lard and the sugar to the cooked rice. Mix well until the rice is thoroughly coated.

2 Brush a 900ml/1½ pint mould or pudding basin with the remaining lard. Cover the bottom and sides with a layer of the rice mixture. Mix together the raisins and nuts, and then arrange over the rice.

3 Cover with a thick layer of rice and fill the centre with the chestnut purée. Cover with the remaining rice and flatten the top. Unmould carefully on to a plate and decorate the top with the cherries, angelica and dates. Replace the mould over the pudding, turn over and remove the plate. Cover with a pleated circle of greaseproof paper secured with string.

4 Steam the pudding for 1 hour. Just before it is ready, make the syrup. Dissolve the sugar in the water in a small pan and bring to the boil. Blend the cornflour with 2 tablespoons of water. Add to the pan and simmer gently, stirring until thickened. Invert the pudding on to a serving plate, pour over the syrup and serve immediately.

PREPARATION: 25 MINUTES
COOKING: 1 HOUR
SERVES: 6-8

PEKING TOFFEE APPLES

Pa ssu ping kou

| 125g/4oz plain flour |
| 1 egg |
| 100ml/3½ fl oz water, plus 2 tablespoons |
| 4 crisp apples, peeled, cored and thickly sliced |
| sunflower oil for deep-frying, plus 1 tablespoon |
| 6 tablespoons sugar |
| 3 tablespoons golden syrup |

4 Add the fried apples to the syrup and coat all over. Remove with a perforated spoon and drop quickly into a bowl of iced water. Remove the toffee apples immediately and serve.

1 In a bowl, mix together the flour, egg and 100ml/3½ fl oz of the water, blending thoroughly to make a smooth batter. Dip each piece of apple into the batter.

3 Put the sugar and the remaining water and oil in a clean pan. Dissolve the sugar over gentle heat, stirring constantly. Add the golden syrup and boil to the hard crack stage – 151°C/304°F on a sugar thermometer. The syrup should form brittle threads when dropped into iced water.

2 In a wok or deep frying pan, heat the oil for deep-frying to 180°C/350°F, or until a cube of bread turns brown in 30 seconds. Add the battered apple pieces and deep-fry for 2 minutes until golden. Remove with a perforated spoon and drain on absorbent kitchen paper.

PREPARATION:
15 MINUTES
COOKING: 20 MINUTES
SERVES: 4

GARNISHES, RICE AND SAUCES

PLAIN RICE

350g/12oz long-grain rice
750ml/1¼ pints water

Wash and rinse the rice in cold water, and then drain. Fill a saucepan with the water and bring to the boil over high heat. Add the washed rice and bring back to the boil. Cover the pan tightly with a lid and reduce the heat to a simmer. Cook gently for 20 minutes. Turn off the heat and leave the rice in the covered pan for another 10 minutes to dry out and avoid stickiness. Fluff the rice up with a fork before serving. Serves 4-6.

CLEAR STOCK
Qing tang

1kg/2lb chicken pieces
750g/1½lb pork spareribs
50g/2oz fresh ginger root, unpeeled and cut into chunks
4-5 spring onions
2.75 litres/5 pints water
50ml/2 fl oz Chinese rice wine or dry sherry

Trim off the excess fat from the chicken and pork, and then place in a large saucepan with the ginger and spring onions. Pour in the water and bring to the boil.

Skim off any scum on the surface and then reduce the heat slightly. Cook, uncovered, for at least 1½-2 hours. Leave to cool. When cold, skim off any surface fat with a perforated spoon.

Strain the stock and return to a clean saucepan. Add the rice wine or sherry and bring back to the boil.

Simmer for 5 minutes before using. The stock can be stored in a covered container in the refrigerator for 4-5 days. Makes 2 litres/3½ pints

Note: This stock can be used as the base for a clear soup. Just add 2 teaspoons finely chopped onions, 1 tablespoon light soy sauce and 1 teaspoon salt for every 600ml/1 pint of stock.

SPRING ONION TASSELS

spring onions

To make these tassels, trim the white ends and green leaves of the spring onions so that they are 7.5cm/3 inches long. Cut along each one lengthways through the stalk several times to within 4cm/1½ inches of the end. Place the spring onions in a bowl of iced water for 1 hour until the onions open up. Use as a garnish for Chinese dishes.

MANDARIN PANCAKES
Bo bing

500g/1lb plain flour
300ml/½ pint boiling water
a little vegetable oil

Sift the flour into a mixing bowl. Mix the boiling water with 1 teaspoon of oil, and then slowly stir into the flour with a wooden spoon. Knead the mixture until you have a firm dough, and then divide into 3 equal portions. Roll each portion into a long 'sausage', and then cut each

sausage into 8 equal pieces.

Press each piece into a flat pancake with the palm of your hand. Brush one pancake with a little oil, and then place another on top to form a 'sandwich'. Repeat with the remaining dough to make 12 sandwiches.

Flatten each sandwich into a 15cm/6-inch circle with a rolling pin on a lightly floured surface. Place an ungreased frying pan over moderate heat and, when it is very hot, cook the sandwiches, one at a time. Turn them as soon as air bubbles appear on the surface. Cook the other side until little brown spots appear underneath. Remove from the pan and peel the 2 layers apart. Serve warm with Roast Peking Duck (see page 66). Makes 24 pancakes.

QUICK SWEET AND SOUR SAUCE

2 garlic cloves, crushed
1 tablespoon oil
2 tablespoons light soy sauce
2 tablespoons clear honey
2 tablespoons wine vinegar
2 tablespoons tomato purée
2 teaspoons chilli sauce
2 teaspoons Chinese wine or sherry
2 teaspoons cornflour

Stir-fry the garlic in the oil for 2 minutes and then stir in all the remaining ingredients except the cornflour. Mix the cornflour with a little cold water and stir into the sauce. Bring to the boil, stirring, and then cook for 2 minutes. Serves 4.

SPICY DIPPING SAUCE

2 tablespoons peanut butter
2 teaspoons soy sauce
1 teaspoon red chilli oil
2 teaspoons chicken stock
1 garlic clove, crushed

Mix all the ingredients together and blend well to make a spicy dipping sauce for won tons, dumplings and spring rolls. This sauce will serve 4 people.

CHINESE GARNISHES

The Chinese have always used attractive garnishes of vegetables and fruit to enhance the texture, colour, flavour and appearance of their dishes, particularly on formal occasions. Here are some ideas that you can try out yourself at home.

RADISH ROSES

You will need several fresh, unblemished radishes. Cut off the root end and trim the top of each radish. With a sharp knife, cut thin petals around the sides, starting at the stem end and finishing at the root.

Plunge the radishes into iced water and leave for 1 hour. Drain and pat dry before using as a garnish.

TOMATO LILIES

You will need 2 or 3 firm, red tomatoes which are not too large. Insert a sharp knife into the side of the tomato at an angle and then work around the tomato, making 'V' cuts as you go. Carefully separate the 2 halves, and you will have 2 attractive lily shapes. Repeat with the other tomatoes.

TOMATO ROSES

Alternatively, you can make tomato roses as a garnish. Using a sharp knife, peel off the skin, like an apple, in one piece, working from the top to the bottom of the tomato. Curl the skin into a circle and then invert it.

CUCUMBER CARTWHEELS

Take a small cucumber and using a sharp knife or potato peeler, cut small strips vertically from the peel from one end of the cucumber to the other at 1cm/$\frac{1}{2}$-inch intervals. Remove the cut peel and discard. Slice the cucumber thinly.

CUCUMBER TWISTS

Alternatively, slice the cucumber thinly, leaving on the skin. Make one cut in each slice towards the centre, but not all the way through. Twist both edges of the cucumber in opposite directions. You can make lemon twists in the same way.

LEMON BUTTERFLIES

Take a firm, evenly coloured lemon and cut into thin slices horizontally. Cut out a quarter of the slice on each side to make a butterfly shape, leaving the centre intact. Use to decorate sweet or savoury dishes.

INDEX